Four Seasons with God
Oneness

Haiku Poems

by Keith Kennedy

キース・ケネディ©2015

印刷　アメリカ合衆国
翻訳　株式会社　スタジオメイ　　山崎 望美
写真とデザインはキース・ケネディによるものである。

無断複写・転載を禁じます。この出版物のいかなる部分も、複製、検索システムへの保管、または発行や著者の事前の許可なしにいかなる形式またはいかなる手段によっても引用することができません。これらの用語の外に再生に関するお問い合わせは、出版社にお問い合わせください。

© 2015 by Keith Kennedy

Printed in the United States of America
Translation by Nozomi Yamazaki and Studio May Co., Ltd
Photography and design by Keith Kennedy

All rights reserved. No part of this publication may be reproduced, stored in a retrieval system, or transmitted in any form or by any means without the prior permission of the publishers or authors. Enquiries concerning reproduction outside those terms should be sent to the publishers.

neutrinopub@aol.com
ISBN 978-0-9938035-2-9

四季　神とともに
　　調和

目次 Contents

謝辞 Acknowledgements　　　　　　　　　　xi
はじめに Introduction　　　　　　　　　　　xv

春 Spring

1.	神 God	23
2.	光 Light	24
3.	空 Sky	25
4.	花 Blossom	26
5.	贈り物 Gift	27
6.	自然 Nature	28
7.	礎(いしずえ) Foundation	29
8.	融合 Unity	30
9.	メロディ Melody	31
10.	天蓋 Canopy	32
11.	天国 Heaven	33
12.	祝福 Blessing	34
13.	草原 Meadow	35
14.	美しさ Beauty	36
15.	ちから Power	37
16.	瞬間 Moment	38
17.	生れ変わり Rebirth	39
18.	絵 Picture	40
19.	魂(こころ) Spirit	41
20.	誕生 Born	42

夏 Summer

21.	日差し Sunshine	45
22.	微笑(えみ) Laughter	46
23.	主の恵 Grace	47
24.	うた Song	48
25.	シカ Deer	49
26.	薔薇 Rose	50
27.	樫 Oak	51
28.	乾き Drought	52
29.	バレエ Ballet	53
30.	祈り Prayer	54
31.	デイジー Daisy	55
32.	慈み Kindness	56
33.	蜜 Nectar	57
34.	ソナタ Sonata	58
35.	影 Shadow	59
36.	導き Beacon	60
37.	変化 Change	61
38.	信仰 Faith	62
39.	星 Star	63
40.	月 Moon	64

秋 Fall

41.	橋 Bridge	67
42.	静謐 Serenity	68
43.	忍耐 Endurance	69
44.	コスモス Cosmos	70
45.	どんぐり Acorn	71
46.	雨 Rain	72
47.	一体感 Oneness	73
48.	カボチャ Pumpkin	74
49.	虹 Rainbow	75
50.	谷 Valley	76
51.	岩 Rock	77
52.	心 Heart	78
53.	雲 Cloud	79
54.	意識 Sense	80
55.	地球 Earth	81
56.	旅 Journey	82
57.	サンクチュアリ Sanctuary	83
58.	思いやり Compassion	84
59.	神託 Trust	85
60.	霧 Mist	86

冬 Winter

61.	霜 Frost		89
62.	湖 Lake		90
63.	樺の木 Birch		91
64.	聖書 Scripture		92
65.	雪 Snow		93
66.	ひろがり Ripple		94
67.	森林地帯 Woodland		95
68.	通り道 Gateway		96
69.	潜望鏡 Periscope		97
70.	足跡 Footprint		98
71.	小川 Stream		99
72.	知恵 Wisdom		100
73.	毛布 Blanket		101
74.	露の滴 Dewdrop		102
75.	福音書 Gospel		103
76.	羅針盤 Compass		104
77.	愛 Love		105
78.	神感 Inspiration		106
79.	平和 Peace		107
80.	芳香 Fragrance		108
	参照 Bibliography		111

謝辞
Acknowledgements

謝辞

神は自然を通してご自身を明らかにしています。すべてのものは神によって創られために、地球上で見えるものと天にあり見えないものとがあります。この自然の美しさとシンプルさは、神を讃える私たちの心、そしてこの俳句調の詩に共通している一体感でもあります。

この本は、本質的に神の美への賛歌です。キリストの愛と深遠さに満ちた御言葉についてご教示くださった以下の指導者の方々に心から感謝申し上げます。

ケン重松博士、牧師
ドン・コウイー牧師
ニッキーガンベル牧師
エイビン・ハラルドセイ牧師
森章牧師
トーマス・デイビス牧師

この俳句の出版に方向性を与え賜うた皆様のキリストへの愛に心より感謝申し上げます。

キリストに祝福。

Acknowledgements

God reveals Himself through nature. For all things were created by Him, both visible on earth and invisible in heaven. This beauty and simplicity of nature leads our hearts in praise to God, a sense of oneness that provided the foundation for this haiku poem collection.

This book is a celebration of God's beauty in nature. My thanks and appreciation go to the following inspiring leaders for their profound words and love of Christ:

Dr. Rev. Ken Shigematsu
Pastor Don Cowie
Rev. Nicky Gumbel
Pastor Eyvind Haraldseid
Pastor Akira Mori
Pastor Thomas Davis

Their love for Christ provided direction for this haiku publication to which I offer my gratitude.

Blessings in Christ.

はじめに
Introduction

はじめに Introduction

　神と俳句は一見互いに遠くに見えるかもしれませんが、神も俳句も一体感という視覚的イメージを持っています。「百聞は一見にしかず」という格言を取り上げても一つという概念が表現されていることがわかります。
　これは、イエス・キリストが「私を見た者は父を見たのだ」と言われたようにということです（ヨハネ 14：9、新国際版）。この聖句は、紛れもなく父と息子が一体であるとして神の姿を示しています。神の深遠なる御言葉は、人間の心に神の御心で書かれたキリストからの手紙であることを示している（2 コリント 3：3）。私たちの心と神の像に刻まれた神の手紙は、私たちに神の栄光と聖句の中で神が創造したすべてのものを見せてくださいます。像と御言葉としてのキリストのこれらの啓示は、自然の中で神の創造を映しだしているのです。
　トッレは、宇宙はその全体から切り離すことができない存在でありすべての生命が相互に関係していると主張しました（2009）。それゆえ、全ての原子が無限に関連しているように、命（人生）は孤立して存在することはできません。思考の心は、人生の見えるものだけしか見ることができません。そうではないものを考えた場合にのみ、自然の中で調和と神聖の意識に気付くことができます（トッレ、2009）。自然のこのテーマは、神の創造と神の手によるものを詠む俳句の概念とのつながりを帯びています。神が書いたように、新しい天と地の創造を愉しんでください。前者の考えは心に響くことはありませんし忘れることもありません（イザヤ書　65 章 17 節）。自己を忘れ、自然をはるかに超える神の素晴らしさと御心による自然をご覧く

xv

ださい。ひとつのより深い意味は日本の詩人松尾芭蕉の特徴です。

　俳句は、深遠なる筆致でのあらゆるものの有りのままを包含する詩の形式です。独自の17音節の形式は、16世紀頃の日本で始まりました。日本で最も有名な詩人である芭蕉（1644年から1694年）は、自然界の感覚を得るために、自然と親しく語り合うことを旨としていました。簡素、深遠、開放性という芭蕉の原則は、彼の俳句の構造の基礎となりました（マツ、1966）。この深遠と簡素は、人を取り巻くものと茶道のような文化的活動のようなものに注意を引きつける自然のイメージに調和と客観性を伝えています。（2010 パット、ワーケンタイン＆ティル）

　日本では自然環境が一体感とすべての物事の深遠さを反映するように社会を形作ります。私たちは、自然界のあらゆるものの原子とお互いに関係しています。俳句は自然と繋がるためにまばらに細工された単語を使いますが、俳句という詩は必ずしも欧米の視点からの詩ではなくむしろ客観的修辞的表現であります。（1973 安田）

　神の創造に身を委ねてみえる側の生活を越えて観る能力は、紛れもなく神の一体感とを明らかにする。私たちは神の慈愛と満ち溢れる喜びを体験するように創られています。（2013 重松）聖書は多くの神の一体感と奇蹟を示しています。この奇蹟に気付いたことで芭蕉は読者を素晴らしい美しさへの旅、映像と言葉が徐々にひとつになっていく旅へと誘います。あらゆる点でこの人生においての認識が生きるものすべてと響き合い、目を通して理解するほんのわずかな美しさと響き合うのです。（2011 ハーッシュフィールド）私たちが一体であるようには彼らは一つであるという栄光を与えたと神はお告げになられたのです。（ヨハネ書17章22節）

God and haiku may at first glance seem distant from each other, but they both carry the visual image of oneness. Think of the dictum "a picture is worth a thousand words" it expresses the idea of one.

As Jesus said "Anyone who has seen me has seen the father" (John 14:9, New International Version). This scripture undeniably depicts the image of God as one of the father and son. God's profound word shows that we are a letter from Christ written with the Spirit of God on human hearts (2 Corinthians 3:3). His letter inscribed on our hearts and the image of God, help us to behold God's glory and all things created by Him in scripture. These revelations of Christ as the image and the Word reflect His divine creation in nature.

Tolle (2009) argued that the universe is inseparable from its whole and all life is interconnected. Therefore, life cannot exist in isolation as all atoms are infinitely related. The thinking-mind can only see the visible side of life; only when thinking subsides, is awareness of harmony and sacredness apparent in nature (Tolle, 2009). This theme of nature bears witness to God's creation and connects with the concepts of haiku to reveal God's hand at work. As God has written, behold the creation of new heavens and earth. Former thinking will not come to mind nor be remembered (Isaiah, 65:17); forget the self and see the numinous wonders of God and nature at work. A deeper sense of one, a characteristic of the Japanese poet, Matsuo Bashō.

Haiku is a poetic form that embraces all nature on a profound level; its unique 17 syllable form originated in Japan around the 16th century. Japan's most famed poet, Bashō, believed in communing with nature to gain a sense of the natural world (1644-1694). Bashō's principles of simplicity, depth and openness became the basis for his haiku poetry structure (Matsu, 1966). This depth and simplicity convey harmony and objectivity with natural imagery that call attention to one's surroundings and such cultural activities as the tea ceremony (Patt, Warkentyne, & Till, 2010).

In Japan the natural environment shapes society to reflect a oneness and true depth of everything; we are interconnected with the atoms of all things in the natural world. Although haiku utilizes sparsely crafted words to connect with nature, haiku poems are not necessarily poetry from a Western perspective but rather objective imagery (Yasuda, 1973).

The ability to immerse oneself in God's creation and see beyond the visible side of life undeniably reveals His oneness and wonder. We are designed to experience His grace and abundant joy (Shigematsu, 2013).The Bible makes numerous references to God's oneness and wonder. Bashō's awareness of this wonder guides readers along a journey of significant beauty, a journey where images and words fade into one. This awareness of life all around resonates with every living thing, atoms of beauty seen only through the eyes of understanding (Hirshfield, 2011). God said I have given them the glory that they may be one as we are one (John 17:22).

四季　神とともに
　　調和

春
Spring

神 God 1

万物も
季節も神の
愛にあり

創(つく)られた
春夏秋冬(しゅんかしゅうとう)
光(ひ)と闇と

God is everything,
all seasons under His realm.
Immense faithful love.

Spring, summer, fall and
winter. God's creation reaches
beyond light and dark.

光 Light 2

芽吹く春
神の光に
生かされて

万物の
いとなみの時
天の国

Spring season spurts with
God's amazing light, a time
of eloquent life.

Time for everything,
abundant activity,
all under heaven.

四季 神とともに *調和*

空 Sky 3

広い空
昼夜が分かつ
春分に

眩(まばゆ)きは
自然紐とく
神の手に

Expanse of the sky
divided by night and day.
Spring equinox comes.

Nature unfolds a
glorious stage of beauty.
God reveals His hand.

花 Blossom 4

ああ桜
神の美しい
贈り物

浮雲に
鷲空高く
希望満ち

Cherry blossom gifts
from His hand. Scattering joy,
paintings of beauty.

Cushion clouds float by,
soaring eagles on high.
Covenant of hope.

贈り物 Gift 5

御教(みおし)えは
調和もたらす
虹色の春

舞い上がる鳥
山頂は空
栄えあれ

Observe God's words as
gifts of harmony. Spring is,
rainbows of color.

Birds gently hover.
Summit peaks capture the sky,
splendor and glory.

自然 Nature 6

聖(きよ)なる
自然が見せる
御心を

高い木々
地に根を下ろす
岩の如(ごと)

God's divine nature
exhibits power through love.
His promise and hope.

Tall trees anchored in
the ground, feeding from below.
Solid as a rock.

四季 神とともに *調和*

礎(いしずえ) Foundation 7

神の愛
感じて強い
永遠(とわ)の人生(ひび)

主を求め
希望の泉
神の愛

Strength comes from knowing
His love. Foundation for life,
forever in Him.

Thirst after the Lord,
He is the fountain of hope.
God is love for all.

融合 Unity 8

日々生きる
絆ひとつに
キリストと

鳥謳う
陽光(ひかり)讃えよ
音楽(おと)奏で

Strands of life bound in
unity. Firmly planted
foundation in Christ.

Delightful song birds,
praise the sunshine from above.
Melodic music.

四季 神とともに *調和*

メロディ Melody 9

静寂の歌
平和を描き
愛あふれ

雨静か
葉にしみいりし
神の滴

Serene melody,
portrays an oasis of
peace, abound in love.

Rain falls silently.
Leaves absorb moisture
from God's water droplets.

天蓋 Canopy 10

恵みの雨
命育む
森の下

いつくもの
人生護(まも)る
森の覆(ふく)

Nourishing rain seeps
deep into forest floors. To
animate growth.

Multitude of life.
Forest canopy protects
smaller animals.

天国 Heaven 11

歓びの
春の力で
森育つ

天の恵み
種と草木に
神の知恵

Spring rejoices in
sync to release energy.
A nurtured forest.

Heaven's showers bring
sustenance to seeds and plants.
God's noble beauty.

祝福 Blessing 12

恵まれた
春の約束
とくべつの色

愛を知る
聖なる場所(ところ)
安らかに

His blessed promise
seen in spring. Brilliant hues
of crested colors.

Love is measured by
the heart, a sanctuary
of safety within.

四季 神とともに *調和*

草原 Meadow 13

草原の.
春に平和の
歌ひびく

そよ風や
かぐわしい花
ひとつなる

Grassy fields of green.
Peaceful meadows of song in
spring, joyful nature.

Breathe the gentle air,
aromatic flowers draw
senses into one.

美しさ Beauty 14

風に舞う
春の花の美
神のわざ

真の愛
知恵の言葉に
心ふるえ

Spring flowers dance in
the breeze. God's significant
beauty resonates.

His love expressed through
truth. Inscribed words of wisdom,
striking gentle hearts.

四季 神とともに *調和*

ちから Power 15

聖書より
魂(こころ) の平和
神の愛

沈黙に
のみ知恵ありき
御国(くに)で知り

Scripture invades the
mind. Images of peace flow
to the soul. God's love.

Wisdom seen only
when the noise subsides. Enter
His realm and witness.

瞬間 Moment 16

生ける瞬間(とき)
過ぎ去りし日を
いま学ぶ

たゆまなく
神がもたらす
地上の美

Live in the moment,
experience today for
yesterday has gone.

The realm of God rests
in His right hand. Let fields of
beauty fall on earth.

四季 神とともに *調和*

生れ変わり Rebirth 17

地が温み
春の息吹が
湧きあがる

蜂群れて
陽は葉を射抜く
神の産物(もの)

Earth becomes warmer.
Rebirth of spring into a
frenzy of movement.

Buzzing bees swarm high.
Sunlight pierces between leaves,
God's creatures explore.

絵 Picture 18

虹の彩(いろ)
葉に揺らめいて
春に萌ゆ

絶景に
空輝いて
山 遜(へりくだ)る

Shimmer of colors
on iridescent leaves. Warm
air nurtures atoms.

Picture perfect sight,
sparkling under the sunny
sky. Mountains bow down.

四季 神とともに *調和*

魂(こころ) Spirit 19

春嬉し
わが魂や
神のもと

山頂(やま)超えて
愛つくる季節(とき)
今讃え！

Enjoy spring with God,
seat of our spiritual life.
Glimpse at His wonder.

Beyond mountain peaks,
descending love creates a new
season. Rejoice now!

誕生 Born 20

新たな日
春から夏へ
移りゆく

弾む心
カモメは歌う
命の海

A new day arrives,
spring changes into summer.
Bountiful array.

Spiritual souls cheer.
Seagulls sing aloud, oceans
full of active life.

四季 神とともに 調和

夏
Summer

日差し Sunshine 21

溢れる日差し
植物茂り
夏来たる

神描く
喜び讃え
御言葉を

Bountiful sunshine.
Flurry of plant growth emerges
as summer prevails.

God's painted image.
Exalt His name, sing with joy.
Always share His word.

微笑(えみ) Laughter 22

神の微笑(えみ)
暖静の空
夏の青

神の香
瞬間(とき)流れゆく
つつまれて

God's laughter enfolds,
warm serene skies project
blue hues of summer.

His fragrance catches,
cascading moments of time.
Encased in oneness.

主の恵 Grace 23

力ふたたび
主の恵
平安や

木に鳩の
巣ありて平和
悲喜ともに

Renewal of strength,
miracles and grace abound
in love, peace and joy.

Doves nest atop trees,
emblem of peace. Oneness in
laughter and despair.

うた Song 24

朝日に霧
コオロギ歌う
コンサート

創造の
奇跡の自然
愛つつむ

Misty morning sun.
Crickets singing noisily,
a chirping concert.

Nature adorned in
miracles of creation,
love wrapped in sunlight.

四季 神とともに 調和

シカ Deer 25

赤シカの狩り
ウサギ森の葉に
もぐる夏！

吠える犬
神の荒野に
みな共に

Creative red deer
hunt, rabbits burrow into
forest leaves. Summer!

Neighboring dogs bark.
God's wilderness united,
species together.

薔薇 Rose 26

蕾ある
棘の茎もつ
あでやかさ

朝の薔薇
露花びらに
御心のまま

Buds atop thorny
stems, protected elegant
beauty in color.

Morning summer rose,
dew drops on petals of love,
everything in Him.

四季 神とともに *調和*

樫 Oak 27

樫の木や
森にそびえる
安らぎの

神の保護
求める者へ
安寧の時

Magnificent oaks,
conquerors of the forest.
Shelter and refuge.

God's protection for
those who seek. Aromatic
moments of safety.

乾き Drought 28

乾きさえ
神が心を
満たしゆく

夏の雨
植物潤い
よみがえる

Unexpected drought,
God replenishes empty
hearts. Nature hydrates.

Summer rain quenches
thirsty plants. Vitality
returns with power.

四季 神とともに *調和*

バレエ Ballet 29

スズメ舞う
森の宴に
神踊る

花のワルツ
調和と愛に
祈りかな

Sparrows dance in tune,
forest concert for nature.
A divine ballet.

Flowers waltz for Christ.
Harmony and love, rejoice
in prayer for Him.

祈り Prayer 30

跪き
感謝し祈る
神の愛

夏は来ぬ
共に味わう
キツネらも

Bow to the Lord, pray
in thanks. Celebrate immense
kindness and pure love.

Summer blooms, time for
banquets and sharing. Foxes
feast on sweet berries.

デイジー Daisy 31

小花揺れ
彩なるヒナギク
空の下

クモゆるり
鳥から逃れ
神の愛！

Petite flowers wave,
colorful daisies express
thanks. Below warm skies.

Spiders crawl slowly,
escaping watchful eyes of
hungry birds. God loves!

慈み Kindness 32

教書告ぐ
調和の喜び
慈しむ

慈愛満ち
生けるもの似て
ありがたき

Pastoral letters
written, harmonious joy.
Green paths nurture love.

Tender kindness grows,
plants and animals alike.
Give thanks and receive!

四季 神とともに *調和*

蜜 Nectar 33

神の蜜
魂の糧
愛に自由

調和のリズム
自然が示す
景色や音

God's nectar, words of
enrichment for caring souls.
Taste freedom in love.

Rhythms of oneness.
Nature defines direction,
share the sights and sounds.

ソナタ Sonata 34

日が没み
涼しき夜に
生きるもの

月明かり
森のソナタが
神讃え

Sunset falls, cool night
awakens nocturnal life.
Animals feasting.

Adorned in moonlight,
forest sonata begins.
Rejoice His presence.

四季 神とともに *調和*

影 Shadow 35

月の影
荒野に光
葉の下に虫

神与ふ
くらしに和あり
幸ありて

Moonlight casts shadows,
wilderness seeks light. Insects
crawl beneath moist leaves.

God provides for all,
life exists within oneness.
Happiness abound.

導き Beacon 36

希望の光
信者導く
暗闇を

神求め
永遠の愛
心より！

Hilltop light of hope,
beacons guide lost believers.
Safety in darkness.

Seek God in pastures,
everlasting love endures.
Open your heart, pray!

四季 神とともに 調和

変化 Change 37

季節変わり
温(ぬく)まる夜も
ありのまま

夏の日短く
描く涼しさ
色の技

Seasonal change takes
hold. Warm nights dissolve into
pristine lit landscapes.

Summer days shorten.
Coolness drives variety,
colors reveal art.

信仰 Faith 38

信仰に
季節移ろい
行く未来

神の偉業(わざ)
山々みせる
自然の彫刻

Faith transcends borders.
Seasons transform, divine power
shapes human future.

God's stunning marvel,
mountains compel beholders,
nature's rock sculptures.

星 Star 39

夜の闇
ダイヤ煌き
陽は休む

知恵光る
星の瞬き
あちこちで

Night supersedes day,
sky diamonds shine bright alone,
sun rests in slumber.

Wisdom on beams of
celestial light. Stars gleam
everywhere in sight.

月 Moon 40

月夜冴え
秋なお抱く
夏の色

神ありき
紅葉にきらり
その姿

Cool clear night reveals
moonlight. Fall begins holding
back summer's colors.

God's omnipresence,
red and yellow colored leaves,
gleaming art image.

四季 神とともに 調和

秋
Fall

四季 神とともに *調和*

橋 Bridge 41

葉の色に
鳥のさえずり
神の技

愛に在り
創造の架け橋
知恵包む

Birds tweet among fall
leaves. Palette of seasonal
color, God's artwork.

Love abound through His
presence. Bridging creation
to enfold wisdom.

静謐 Serenity 42

平和待つ
神の御言葉
深紅の秋

高い木は
暖気にとどく
森の静

Peace awaits God's word.
Fall foliage displays hues
of deep vivid red.

Tall trees reach for warm
air. Serenity reigns through
forests everywhere.

忍耐 Endurance 43

愛耐えて
力讃えよ
神の恵み

花散るも
御言葉は永遠
代々に

Love endures trials,
blessing source of energy.
Unique gift of grace.

Flowers change and fall.
God's word survives forever
through generations.

コスモス Cosmos 44

羽色の葉
花は輝く
秋の色

幸せな
コスモス踊る
一面に

Pinnate color leaves,
blooming radiant heads, fall
eagerly appears.

Happy cosmos dance.
Seasonal annuals galore,
countryside carpet.

四季 神とともに *調和*

どんぐり Acorn 45

空腹に
どんぐり拾って
リスの秋

天の下
荒野の実り
命の糧

Hungry scavengers
retrieve fallen acorn nuts.
Squirrel's fall delight.

Food for life under
heaven. Feasting wilderness
receives sustenance.

雨 Rain 46

天の涙
動植物を
潤し響く

自然が見せる
父なる平和
一体感

Tears from heaven, God
waters plants and animals.
Drumming rain drops.

Nature unveils love,
oneness with Him, images
of fatherly peace.

四季 神とともに *調和*

一体感 Oneness 47

喜びは
自然と神と
共にあり

松揺れて
つがいのカササギ
終の愛

Fragments of joy yield
a sense of oneness. Nature
and God together.

Scattered pine trees sway,
magpies perched atop in pairs.
Love is always kind.

カボチャ Pumpkin 48

神の愛
かぼちゃも実り
豊かな季節

青空に
リンゴは熟す
陽の園で

God's harvest of love,
fall pumpkins galore. Season
for bountiful crops.

Basking under blue
skies, sunlight ripens apples
up and down orchards.

四季 神とともに *調和*

虹 Rainbow 49

雨曲げる
光に色の
滴かな

虹つくる
神のキャンバス
魂に

Sun rays and rain in
unison, refracted light
and color droplets.

Rainbow creation,
stunning canvas from God. Art
to inspire lost souls.

谷 Valley 50

鷲高く
エデンの園へ
希望と誉

神の谷
木潤す雨
喜びに

Eagles soar above,
secrete garden of Eden.
Hope and grace in Him.

Trees refreshed with rain,
valleys planted by God. Joy
to experience.

岩 Rock 51

落ち葉舞う
キリストが立つ
谷の岩

内なる美
自然を感じる
強き心

Fall winds twirl fallen
leaves. Valley rocks symbolize
His might, stand on Christ.

Glimpse at nature for
the soul's view. Inner beauty
and spiritual strength.

心 Heart 52

神求め
救われ真の
強さ得る

平安に
大きな喜び
永遠の愛

Troubled hearts seek God, mind and spirit saved. Ageless truth and strength within.

Trails that guide inner peace. Unspeakable joy and everlasting love.

雲 Cloud 53

虹の雲
地上の神託
ありがたき

王護り
命が受ける
知と誉

Fluffy rainbow clouds,
His covenant over earth.
Covered joyfulness.

Noble king protects,
every living thing receives.
Wisdom and glory.

意識 Sense 54

秋が来る
動物たちに
冷えた夜

北風に
葉は舞い落ちる
神のもと

Fall rhythm alters,
animals sense seasonal
change. Cool nights set in.

Northerly winds blow,
leaves descend beautifully. God
sheds grace everywhere.

四季 神とともに *調和*

地球 Earth 55

気流逃げ
陽が赤道超え
昼縮む

冬至から
リズムは変わり
冬眠に

Air currents escape,
sun crosses earth's equator.
Days become shorter.

Sleepy solstice starts,
circadian rhythms change.
Animals retire.

旅 Journey 56

神の愛
関わりの旅
復活求め

自然織る
暮らしのリズム
神の愛

Discerning God's love,
journey of relationship.
Seek restoration.

Nature's planned rhythm,
connected with life. Seasons
change, His love remains.

サンクチュアリ Sanctuary 57

避難する
山の聖域
神まねく！

自然の地
アナグマ、ウサギ
神護る

Shelter from weather,
mountain sanctuary for
safety. God beckons!

Nature's habitat,
badgers and rabbits escape
cold winds, He protects.

思いやり Compassion 58

好意が信を
共感が長い
関係を

神の国
愛は寛容
いつの日も！

Kindness creates trust,
compassion develops life
long relationships.

Under His kingdom,
love is always forgiving.
Every season!

神託 Trust 59

石の御言葉
平和と信の
真あり

新たな愛
護り励ます
命なら

His word carved on stone,
tablets of truth and value.
Peace and trust unite.

Renewed strength of love.
Refuge and encouragement,
life essential traits.

霧 Mist 60

朝霧に
動物眠る
寒い冬

群れる鳥
神が与える
思いやり

Morning mist prevails.
Fall hides behind winter chills,
inactive animals sleep.

Birds flock together,
scarcity of food. God gives
compassionately.

四季 神とともに 調和

冬
Winter

四季 神とともに *調和*

霜 Frost 61

雁は南へ
湖畔に初霜
侘しき地

冬枯れて
鳥去りて知る
ああ神よ

Geese flock south, first frost
blankets suburban lakesides.
Taunted barren land.

Winter strips away
life. Pounding forces diffuse,
praise God for changes.

湖 Lake 62

湖上の鳥が
魚とる
冬の地平線

氷上に
水のスライド
ひんやりと

Fish surface for food,
birds glide over lakes. Seasons
change, winter skyline.

Crystal clear mirrored
image, slide show on water.
Cold beauty in sync.

樺の木 Birch 63

月明かり
銀色の樺
きらめいて

樹の香り
古代の聖書
紐解いて

Moonlight birch trees stand
tall, silver beauties of night.
Shimmering collage.

Resinous fragrance,
ancient scriptures on majestic
bark. Scrolls of history.

聖書 Scripture 64

聖なる書
パピルスにある
愛と真実

聖書告ぐ
生きるものへの
知恵ともに

Sacred writings, God's
Word on ancient papyrus.
Inscribed truth and love.

Scriptural guidance,
His perfect plan for living.
Knowledge and oneness.

雪 Snow 65

　　北の青空
　　雪しんしんと
　　地を覆う

　　地が緩み
　　鳥が餌得るも
　　神の意図

Arctic steel blue skies,
snowflakes dispersed silently.
Sparsely covered land.

Warm ground melts. Relief
for birds, feeding continues.
His plan for creatures.

ひろがり Ripple 66

雪どけが
渇きをいやす
生き物の

冬の希望
命を救う
歓喜の地

Melted snow, water
droplets ripple. Refreshing
thirsty animals.

Winter's cup of hope,
life saving. Irrigated
earth expresses joy.

森林地帯 Woodland 67

プラタナスの川、
嵐近づく
東風

きゃしゃな枝
凍える生物（もの）が
庇護求む

Sycamore trees creek,
storm approaches. Easterly
wind howls through bushes.

Spindly branches break,
temperature drops. Wildlife
seeks hope and cover.

通り道 Gateway 68

冬が来る
枯れ木導く
閉ざされし地

神の地に
旅人休む
その一夜

Winter gateway opens,
bare trees reveal path ahead.
Hidden enclosure.

God's sanctuary,
bewildered travelers rest,
overnight cover.

四季 神とともに *調和*

潜望鏡 Periscope 69

枯れ木ゆえ
潜望鏡に
聖なる景色

白い峰
その美しさ
神の作

Bare land yields clear view,
periscopic look through His
natural wonder.

Distant snow-capped peaks.
Scenic beauty created,
God's faithful design.

足跡 Footprint 70

暗い道
雪の足跡
かすかな光

天使招く
冬への旅
雪ふわり

Dark slippery path.
Hikers leave snowy footprints,
barely enough light.

Holy angels guide.
Inward journey of winter,
snowflakes kissing ground.

四季 神とともに *調和*

小川 Stream 71

せせらぎに
小さき命(もの)が
地を満たす

天の恵み
めぐり来る冬、
いま讃え

Living water streams,
flowing molecules of life.
Replenishing earth.

God's gift from heaven.
Nature's unfolding winter,
His glory on earth.

知恵 Wisdom 72

命とは
知恵を授かる
愛の川

神の庇護
天の清らかさ
安らぎの

Understanding lives
in knowledge, God gives wisdom.
Flowing streams of love.

His mystery guards.
Purity from heaven,
spiritual safety.

毛布 Blanket 73

雪覆う
白樺の木の
美しさ

吹く風も
地上のすべて
神のもと

Blanket of snow, white
birch stands, winter exhibits
beautiful visions.

Cold wind exudes force,
nature's grip on planet earth.
All under God's realm.

露の滴 Dewdrop 74

朝の陽に
消えゆく滴
誰も知らず

短くも
いかなるときも
愛に生き

Early morning sun,
dewdrops scatter unaware,
simply passing through.

Short life existence,
enjoy every moment. In
love, imparting life.

福音書 Gospel 75

キリストの
奇跡と真実
愛の知恵

幸いに
使徒が御国の
祝福へ

Christ's life and teachings.
Miracles bound in truth. Love
reflects His wisdom.

Servants clothed in grace.
Disciples for His kingdom,
heavenly blessings.

羅針盤 Compass 76

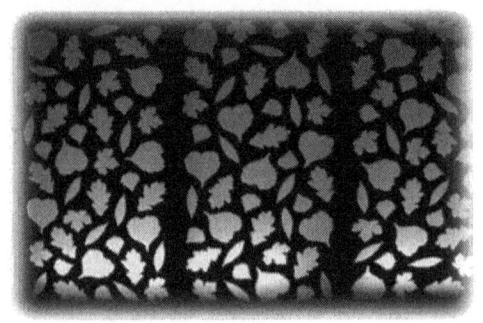

神が指す
良き行いと
良き言葉

光ある
神の不思議は
無限の愛

God's compass directs.
Undeniable goodness,
bound in deeds and words.

His mystery dwells
in light, divine image.
Boundless love on earth.

愛 Love 77

静かな愛
至福の夢を
分かち合う

雨に陽が
祈りでひとつに
永遠に

Quietly love moves
in rhythm. Sharing blissful
dreams beyond reason.

Sunshine on rainy
days. Unity in prayer
with Him forever.

神感 Inspiration 78

わが心
御言葉胸に
自由なり

キリストの
希望は愛を
永遠に

Inspiration holds
His word in hearts. Adrift in
spiritual freedom.

Christ guides visions, hope
enriches everlasting
love eternally.

平和 Peace 79

嵐越え
季節はかわる
平和満ち

芽は息吹き
動物と自然
鳥歌う

Last winter storm, joy
overcomes seasonal change.
Wildlife peace prevails.

Buds start appearing.
Animals and nature thrive,
birds begin singing.

芳香 Fragrance 80

香る花
自然が創る
御心で

春の花
美しい踊り
イエスとともに

Clusters of flowers
exude fragrances. Nature's
craft in His image.

Glorious spring blooms,
dancing heads of beauty. In
oneness with Jesus.

参照
Bibliography

参照

ハーシュフィールド J.（2011） 俳句の心
シアトル、ワシントン州：アマゾンデジタルサービス株式会社

松尾　B.（1966）奥の細道、その他の旅行記（湯浅信之訳）
英国ロンドン　ペンギン社

ケン・シゲマツ(2013) 神は私のすべて：いかに古代のリズムの助けにより、忙しい人々が神に接することができるか。グランドラピッズ、MI ゾンダーバン

エックハルト・トール（2009）生きとし生けるものとの調和：新たな世界からの閃きの選択。ニューヨーク、NY：プルーム

パット・J、ワーケンタイン・M＆ティル B.（2010）
俳句：日本のアートと詩
カリフォルニア州サンフランシスコ：ザクロコミュニケーションズ

安田、K. E.（1973）
日本の俳句：その本質的な自然、歴史、英語での可能性
北クラレンドン、バーモント：タトル出版

ゾンダーバン社(2015)『新国際訳』 聖書(NIV)グランド・ラピッド（ミシガン）ゾンダーバン

Bibliography

Hirshfield, J. (2011). *The heart of haiku.* Seattle, WA: Amazon Digital Services Inc.

Matsuo, B. (1966). *The narrow road to the deep north, and other travel sketches.* (N. Yuasa, Trans.). London, UK: Penguin.

Shigematsu, K. (2013). *God in my everything: How an ancient rhythm helps busy people enjoy God.* Grand Rapids, MI: Zondervan.

Tolle, E. (2009). *Oneness with all Life: Inspirational selections from a new earth.* New York, NY: Plume.

Patt, J., Warkentyne, M., & Till, B. (2010). *Haiku: Japanese art and poetry.* San Francisco, CA: Pomegranate Communications.

Yasuda, K. E. (1973). *Japanese haiku: Its essential nature, history, and possibilities in English.* North Clarendon, VT: Tuttle Publishing

Zondervan. (2015). *NIV Holy Bible.* Grand Rapids, MI: Zondervan.

www.ingramcontent.com/pod-product-compliance
Lightning Source LLC
Chambersburg PA
CBHW030120170426
43198CB00009B/685